PETER DANIELS is the author of four poetry collections and
several pamphlets, including two Poetry Business prizewinners.
He has won poem competitions including the Arvon, *TLS*
and Ledbury, and his translations of Vladislav Khodasevich
from Russian (Angel Classics, 2013) were shortlisted for
three awards including the Oxford-Weidenfeld prize. He
has a Creative Writing PhD from Goldsmiths, London.
As queer writer in residence at the London Metropolitan
Archives he wrote the obscene *Ballad of Captain Rigby*.

T0352918

ALSO BY PETER DANIELS

POETRY

Breakfast in Bed, with Kenneth King and Kieron Devlin
(Oscars Press, 1986)
Peacock Luggage, with Moniza Alvi (Smith/Doorstop, 1992)
Be Prepared (Smith/Doorstop, 1994)
Blue Mice, as Peter Daniels Luczinski, (Vennel Press, 1999)
Through the Bushes, as Peter Daniels Luczinski (Smith/Doorstop, 2000)
Work & Food (Mulfran Press, 2010)
Mr Luczinski Makes a Move (HappenStance, 2011)
Counting Eggs (Mulfran Press, 2012)
The Ballad of Captain Rigby (Personal Pronoun, 2013)
A Season in Eden (Gatehouse Press, 2016)
My Tin Watermelon (Salt, 2019)

TRANSLATIONS

Vladislav Khodasevich, *Selected Poems* (Angel Classics, 2013)

ANTHOLOGIES

Take Any Train: A Book of Gay Men's Poetry (Oscars Press, 1990)
Jugular Defences: An AIDS Anthology, with Steve Anthony
(Oscars Press, 1994)

PETER DANIELS
Old Men

SALT

SHEFFIELD

PUBLISHED BY SALT PUBLISHING 2024

2 4 6 8 10 9 7 5 3 1

Copyright © Peter Daniels 2024

Peter Daniels has asserted his right under the Copyright, Designs and
Patents Act 1988 to be identified as the author of this work.

*This book is sold subject to the condition that it shall not, by way of
trade or otherwise, be lent, resold, hired out, or otherwise circulated
without the publisher's prior consent in any form of binding or cover
other than that in which it is published and without a similar condition
including this condition being imposed on the subsequent publisher.*

First published in Great Britain in 2023 by
Salt Publishing Lt4
18 Churchill Road, Sheffield, S10 1FG United Kingdom
www.saltpublishing.com

Salt Publishing Limited Reg. No. 5293401

A CIP catalogue record for this book is available from the British Library

ISBN 978 1 78463 317 2 (Paperback edition)

Typeset in Sabon by Salt Publishing

Printed and bound in Great Britain by Clays Ltd, Elcograf S.p.A

To my old man
Jason Beazley

Contents

I

Old Keys

Bodily decrepitude is wisdom; young
We loved each other and were ignorant.
W. B. YEATS, 'After Long Silence'

My Dirt

I have it in me. It's a speck of dirt that grows
and lives on pleasure, from down low, inside
my dirty place. It likes that unholy fact.

Lodged in the gland with piss, jism, cum, and
the testosterone it feeds on, its nature is growth.
The pressure of my joy enhances the effect.

Contagious in its way, but not to you, strangely,
though it's so dirty. Its filth is all its own, but it
wants to be mine. The fruit is cursing the fig tree.

It's part of me but not mine yet, little enemy
that makes unknown demands, but fulfils my
demands on myself, my need to be victim.

My dirty soul's expression, it belongs to me
like a sullen servant to fuck me up, a peevish
master to take me over, not because I'm a faggot

but because its wrongness is its character. Any
dirt is matter in the wrong place, revealing
the flaw in its purpose, like a bad vaccination.

When will I know if I've left it behind me? When
is there to know? It may need to be blasted
from the inside out, bleached, scrubbed, vacuumed:

this is speculation, so far. It's there but I don't
know its intentions, or the negotiations still
to come. Let's not talk now of defeat or victory.

City of Mouth

At the same time, if the man indicates his desire for this act,
he first refuses then, having protested, devotes himself to it
                              – *Kama Sutra (trans. Alain Daniélou)*

I watch him turn again at the invitation, here's Dick
Whittington looking at London disdainfully,
not for a gold pavement, but *Oh, look at you, you
losers, I'll give you some genuine dick to suck,
city of pussy boys, city of mouth, city of mine.*

Another dinner for the mayor, rows and rows of mouths,
the committees on drains, committees on prostitution,
gagging with the correct approach: they'll have to refuse
whatever's offered, but doing their job dictates
devotion to the task, once it's been accepted.

Whittingtons were my ancestors: not famous Dick,
he had no descendants, but strapping farm boys ploughing
the soil on the fringes of London, feeding the mouths.
They gave of their fertility till they had to turn
towards the hungry city as it sucked them in.

The city belongs to the one who has awarded himself
the keys: the city of fleas and lumpy mattresses will be
open to his turning. Three more times Lord Mayor
up on the hill with the pussycat rubbing his leg, tail
erect, and his own ambition making him hard again.

East Bedfont

Strange to me that I hadn't noticed
the date, the eve of the fifth anniversary
of my mother's death, the day I chose
to go to the village where she was born
to look around at where her ashes
at last will be deposited like an archive
in a hall of memories: none of them
my memories, but now belonging to me.

Here's the village, now a straggling suburb
out on the edge of it all before the airport,
but nice – you don't notice warehouses
and logistics parks: my gran would be
at home. But she's not here, her ashes
left in Birmingham, where she lived
with us. I was asked my worst influence:
'My grandmother, she spoiled me.'
I was to replace her son, killed in the war,
and her husband, my grandfather –
already long gone, buried at that dead
time I love, the lowest end of winter
not yet spring. In the rich alluvial
Thames Valley soil, the water table's high,
the digging fills quickly, and a coffin
splashes into it. My mother told me how
her mother shuddered at that moment,
a fear seemingly deeper than mourning,
fear of what's not nice for a burial.

I take my photo of the church I've known
from photos – Saxon in origin, altered
and added to over a thousand years,
quirky behind enormous topiary peacocks.
This villagey suburban niceness always
where I was brought up to be, and yet I've
never been here till my mother was dead.
I still try to be nice. I've stopped on the way
to an unrespectable encounter the other
side of the airport, on a day that happens
to be the day before it comes to five years
since my mother's death, and her ashes still
in their unceremonious cardboard box
in the stiff grey paper bag in a corner
of the bedroom, waiting for the soil.

Two Uncles

Johnny was killed at Monte Cassino,
Freddy went down with TB.
They were my uncles but both died young,
they could only meet in me.

After my mother's brother,
they gave me the middle name John:
I knew of Johnny from an early age
especially from my gran.

Freddy was brother to my father,
who never mentioned his name.
I only heard about Freddy
when I was much older than him.

Freddy didn't get his bar-mitzvah
but he was a Jew and a Scotsman.
Johnny's English foreskin was
too tight and needed circumcision.

I exist to replace them,
except I don't know how:
I find my own love for two lost men
I might have resembled now.

A Map

He's at the piano again but he likes most
the look of notes on the page. The music
moves him but he's bashful learning it.

There's a plan to go fishing with his friend,
the bossy one, the only classmate smaller
than he is, but he has no idea about fishing.

He finds the shape of his desire at seven:
a man at a crazy golf course in Brittany,
nipples sharp under a tight white t-shirt.

How what you like moves you on into being
who you've become: he has no idea what
you might need to do to make it happen.

In the long days before growing up, he can
spend the whole time drawing a map
of an elaborate city that will never exist.

When he understands what he can create
he won't have to pretend, but by that time
there may be nothing left to invent.

The Half-Brick

Down the cinder path
    they follow me, victim.
The half-brick hitting
    my back as they laugh.

Or the yellow snow shoved
    down my neck,
and I expect them
    to treat me like this.

Or I'm lying in nettles under
    his wobbly penis while
he tries to piss on me: he
    can't, or decides against.

And I admit I want that
    piss to flow, more nettles
on my skin, the boys
    making the most of it.

Here's my body if you
    want it, want what you
can do to my soul,
    make me suffer.

I'm a posh boy from
    up the road. There's
nothing I can do to
    make them my masters.

Unopened

I think the children smell unopened

                    – Mark Doty, 'No'

The place I came from claimed me back like a dog.
Safety is easy: danger is charm, charm is danger.

And an unopened rose can stay itself, folded
and unavailable, but where a child might come from.

All I could do then, dreaming a man, wanting to know
how to approach: try it the hard way, it's easy.

His roll of silk is embarrassingly small, but
ultimately, it is good luck. Thank you, I Ching.

My dream chemistry, my dogfaced self, my rose heart,
I brought them all back to the place I came from.

Moseley Park

Our dance was out of the closets,
        into the streets.
Birmingham Gay Liberation Front,
        planning the disco
at the Eagle & Tun: *Unless*
        Glen's stereo is made of
anti-matter... (that was Ray).

And indoors, figuring out
        how to do it, two of us,
discovering, making it up.
        Yes, it all happened,
we tell our changed selves,
        changed awkwardly,
like Birmingham now.

The emerging butterflies
        of the hot summer
of nineteen-seventy-six
        can't fly out of
the same chrysalis again.
        We can't eat the same
dubious curries at Saleem's.

Moseley's grand old houses
        enclosed a secret park,
one we couldn't enter
        and didn't know, but
our twenties were as open
        as Cannon Hill,
there for our wandering;

at your flat, performing on
            the wooden fire escape for
each other; swanning around
            Moseley Village with its
green iron-railed toilets,
            ourselves in batik T-shirts,
flares, and platform soles.

Later, we left for London's
            opportunity, changing
and changing differently
            through the years of
watching death around us
            and dodging it through
middle age and beyond.

And we must continue
            being what we were
like the continuing city:
            we're made from those
curries, those clothes: anything
            different is a world
of anti-matter. And today

we enter that park – Ian
            with a key, though now
it's public on Wednesdays.
            We've penetrated this
inner place, hidden like
            our old selves: still
enclosed deep inside us.

Encounters with Ron

Across the room – gay rights conference, Manchester –
Ron's eyes and mine, but no further developments.

Across an electronic platform, forty years later,
our eyes begin to flirt again, a little dirtily, but tender.

He visits: further flirtations, but domestically bound
I remain chaste though frustrated and regretful.

Life is confusing enough. Death now closes on Ron
and will continue closing affairs till there are no more people.

Rings

It fits only on my little finger,
the silver ring my mother made me,
with a malachite stone like a green and stripy
blip in existence. Small, but fat and rounded,
sticking out from my hand's edge
into the world, it feels too exposed
for me to wear, in case it knocks
against something hard. The thin silver
is not too loose, but it turns easily
around my finger. Other people wear
engagement and wedding rings that fold
further into the middle of the hand, on the least-used finger.
Pinky rings show themselves on closed hands
to anyone passing, from the side, from behind.
They can signal in an old-fashioned way:
Victorians read them as 'Not interested in marriage.'
I used to wear a steel ring with a square hole in it, a signal
to myself: I found it in a drawer at work, some kind of
component. I once fell off a bicycle, and it bit
into my flesh. When I gave it up I put it back
in another drawer, at another workplace.
Malachite ring, sitting in a drawer at home,
what's the signal? 'My mother made me
a homosexual.'

Evening Primrose

Telling her story one more bloody time, Sheherezade
finally gets to tell him she's strung him along, fucked him
with her dragonfly mind, each evening stuffing his need
with a fairy dildo – and that seems to be what he was
always wanting, only he wouldn't quite admit it.
I picture this in the gardens of the Alhambra, the most
Arabian place I've been to, reimagined at night
with Arabian people. A place to see before you die.
It's the being determined and open to experience
gets you the grace to survive, if you haven't already
swooned and died lightly in the primrose evening.

I'm back in my mother's garden, with the evening primroses.
I used to take evening primrose oil, which I thought was good for
depression till I found it was St John's wort for that,
and evening primrose is meant for pre-menstrual tension.
I'm watching a dragonfly settling prettily on a primrose,
right way up, but I've recently read an article saying how
female dragonflies land upside-down playing dead,
to avoid being harassed by males. *Sexual death feigning
is one of the rarest behaviors in nature*, it says. Maybe
they've already done their duty to the species, or maybe
they just aren't in the mood and fancy some evening primrose.

Here I am, fucking about with the Arabian Nights which
I've never even read, because I wanted to mash up
Sheherezade with the Kama Sutra – and I've only
browsed in that where I've been drawn to some
captivating titbit. An expert says this translation

is wrongheaded, but it caught my attention: *She is determined to unite him with the instrument she is inserting into his anus.* Could she fill my every orifice with fantasy? Could she recondition my queer spot, till in my flibbertigibbet way I too can settle my soul lightly like a dragonfly on an evening primrose?

Pastoral Interlude

Over those two years, some changes of atmosphere, to find
I loved the sweet ways of his dukedom as I love flowers, not too close.
Now I'd walk my mile home from him, past the park, the dry screams
of the roosting peacocks, but the moon glow was from two years back,

a night it told me: *You can be late for once. Or keep on walking,
the other way from the station.* Secreting some unreliable hormone,
I was climbing up that hill and onto the Heath, into the evening, past
an empty orange balloon and its tackle parked flat on the slope.

I began to notice: breathing the scented breeze took in a drag
of discomfort, crowding my cells. I knew his flowers hurt me, but
still I'd be surprised, and not say 'That's enough'. I felt alone
and free, taking my brief exile briskly through that forest,

meeting now and then a few aimlessly purposeful people,
letting them be. Night blooms with open throats greeted me,
their bee-hungry messages put a scratch in my breath,
and all the soothing ice-creams were now long shut away.

By then the wind was brushing harder for nightfall, dusting us
with invisible agony. I was walking away from a sunset,
a quick impressionistic row of smudges, up that last hill towards
London's orange glow, and the orange moon dangling over St Paul's.

Prodigal Son

In the abandoned bedroom he opened the wardrobe door.

In the wardrobe he found the smooth, the scratchy and the knotty,
    he fondled the horn toggles and velvet buttons, the huge
    coats. The coats welcomed him home.
They were hospitable, started dressing him up in outfits of love,
    waistcoats of impossible desire;
they began to clothe him in ways he could never get away from,
    and he wanted them to be his.
Doors opened on brocaded gowns and suits with satin lapels,
he tried on workmen's overalls appliquéd with stars and moons,
drawerfuls of haberdasher's notions festooned at random on
    gingham smocks;
silver stockings clung to him; long diamanté gloves flecked with
    mud and bodily fluids.
Everything became textile. Time began opening up in pleats.
Moments embroidered themselves, slashed open their sequined
    linings;
the room unzipped its cornice to loosen the pressure.
Plain cotton underwear sauntered along the landings chewing gum
    and cracking knuckles. Where was the pair of jeans he found
    so reliable? Making love with the stair carpet.
Where could he put all this stuff when his mother arrived?
Every space had clothes growing out of it.
Every cupboard and spare suitcase bounced open, spilled satin and
    tweed, tailored bodices, yards of substandard hospital linen;

curtains ran themselves up into ballgowns and sprouted
        ostrich plumes, the towelling bathrobe plumped up,
        kept growing, engulfed the toilet and vanity unit,
finally blocking the hallway and the side door to the fire
        escape.

He began thinking: *Alright, I could eat clothes . . .*

Old Keys

Old keys open strange doors where the dark
dwells in the lock. Entering the front brings you
through to the back where the furniture is
older and stranger. There's a thick brown varnish
chipped, you might imagine, by spurs of cavalrymen
waiting to be undone, away from truth or whatever
they fought for. Their own bodies asked to be
betrayed, but they faced any soul unburdened
behind those doors, overcome by the frantic power
with its affront to virtue passing unchallenged.

Behind those doors the inner chambers gave out
lessons in foreign manners, foreplay for friends
to explore with each other's hands as lovers,
a sovereign remedy for the nagging. This was
freedom, that mattered now, between the furnace
and the ash-pit, with the smoke and the heat
burnt off in what they did overnight. In time
who could care, even indeed over the infernal
eternity in which they were expected to regret
the door that opened them to this way of life.

Versatility

Some of these men are on top, some on the bottom, some
pride themselves that their tastes are totally versatile.

In the interests of balance, we let both sides make themselves
known to each other: no fuss, no blame, no fault.

We don't have to be equal in all of it, it's no shame – though
shame might make the pulse throb and the nerves flutter.

The one on top can flip, it's an available mode to switch
between comfort and punishment, leather and velvet.

Balance: it allows us to walk upright holding the sense
of who we are, neither wrongly rigid nor uselessly fluid.

Mind you, the world isn't fair, as we all know too well.
What about when Earth gets to flip its magnetic field?

Level the random with balance, make equalisation
the steady aim, don't let the state of the universe falter.

We play our part: you can do to me what I can do
back to you, to satisfy with tenderness and with filth.

Cherries and Cheese

PAXMAN: What is another word for
   'cherrypickers' and 'cheesemongers'?
CONTESTANT: Homosexuals?
PAXMAN: No. They're regiments in the British
   Army who will be very upset with you.
University Challenge, 2007

Blessed are the cherrypickers, feeling for the finest.
There's two there now, they know what the score might be.
Of all the ways to find what you need so much,
they turn their fingers to uses God didn't think of,
they are the ones to introduce you to touch.

Blessed are the cheesemongers, finding the ones
that are ready. The cheese is signalling
its ripeness in the air, the gross indecency
of innuendo. How do they warm the pot
for each other? What is their taste in tea?

In the Shower

Welcome to my bathroom where I've invited you
to watch me shower, through the mysterious portal
of a phone. The screen is also showing you showering.
You don't tell me how you've carefully set up your own
phone to display your naked image on my phone, but
mine is positioned where the bathroom windowsill
ducks behind the shower curtain. I've propped it
by its leather case, book-like, angled perfectly to open
my own body like a book for you to peruse, and face
where I stand wet under the shower head while you
in your bathroom, somewhere I've never been,
open your body, unaccustomed, unexplored, soap it
as I soap mine, and we watch each other shower down
whatever held us back, and the water takes it away.

Or Is It Love?

Is he artistic? Is he into shoes? I don't
understand how you're a magnet for desire
from people you wouldn't otherwise
have much to do with. How do you
cope with so much attention – or is it love?

If my heart is made out of steel I won't
blame you for the damage. If your heart
is a flower crushed in the push and pull of
amorous commerce, the world of opportunity
needs to grow you another organ of love.

'I've broken a few hearts', he said, but he
knew his own grief. Well-brought-up
and considerate of others, any leftover
feeling was his own, but hearts often
offer themselves to be broken by love.

Did he really? And what did you do then?
He lived at the top of a block of flats
out on the edge of town. I'll never
see him again. It was perfect, and that
was enough. But that's enough of love.

Is that all? What are you doing with
the rest of your life? Ah well, somewhere
in the distance the dance continues.
The maracas go splish-splosh and the music
goes on across the universe of love.

II

Old Trees

An aged man is but a paltry thing,
A tattered coat upon a stick, unless
Soul clap its hands and sing
                    W.B. YEATS, 'Sailing to Byzantium'

Unknown

Of all the unknown people pouring down the other escalator,
one had to be the perfect soul-partner never encountered,
answering the call of the romantic dirt in his head.
But never mind all that, he'd continue following
whatever the gleam seemed to be.
One day he could answer the door
to a wheelbarrow delivering his whole history,
everything he'd seen or felt
and what was worked out from the evidence.
Then he might understand what it was
the wink in the street would have led to,
what the idol of his kind was offering,
who must by statistical evaluation have been for him
the one answering the right question, if he'd thought of it.

Strawberries

Strike me with lightning, see if it makes me happy?
Relying on happenstance might be a drawback.

Even if time and place are right, I can't expect miracles,
or perfect strawberries. I always expect trouble.

I'm a happy pessimist – I dance to the world's joy
with a faltering foot. Life is meant to be terrible.

But when I reach the moment of satisfaction, I can be
happy as a pig with a face full of strawberries.

I enjoy making jam, too: strawberry always the most
difficult – how to keep the flavour so adorable.

The thing is, happiness is the instant it happens.
Perhaps it's ready, but like fruit it can't ever be durable.

Big

You see me from a new place
        opening opportunities,
        the big beginning.

You offer me half an orange
        with the flavour
        that penetrates.

Your mouth and my mouth
        begin to be the right
        angle for the kiss.

Your lips open, our tongues
        penetrate a place
        with a big horizon.

We taste the splash of salt,
        the beginning of
        each other's ocean.

Old Men

Old men in one another's arms, as if we were
unageing, the flesh as good as ever: but love
gets made in its own fashion, and so we
claim each other's body for each other.

What do we depend on? Bread rises for us
and it fills us. We plant potatoes, making
more potatoes, where we think they'll flourish.
We feed on what we have to feed each other.

It all began too late for us, but what we hold
offers this lifetime more than making do:
we make each other real enough to touch,
with time to spend where we complete each other.

The Others

The others, always there, they call us to attention, and they
take our time, they borrow what we owe each other

and we've spent it.

I've been spending more of that than you have, which hurts.
Each other's others take whatever makes them happy, but

it makes us difficult.

Yours are mostly your own flesh and blood, fish and chips,
the house you built. Mine have come with only flesh,

here a mouth, there a finger.

What do we tell each other, what can we give back for whatever
we've desired, and keep the faith we have already? We know

other people hold us to our promise.

A Metaphor

If old men are trees they may have thighs like
tree limbs, while they have hearts of human muscle
beating and beating. They have grown their own
knotted and cross-grained ways, but they are
gentle gentlemen waving arms in the breeze
to attract each other. They can share their
pollen with no care for whose nose it bothers
because they are trees. What they have understood
is their own business and hard to explain, except
being trees they know one day they may become
hollow, and rot before they're cut down, but
they keep on growing. If old men need a picture
of who they are, being literal-minded, maybe
they need to be trees to show how they have
twisted their trunks into a figure: but they aren't,
they're old men with blood and guts and fingers
and faces, bodies that are nothing like trees.

Freedom

I called up the god unaware, and set him free.
His ancient tree didn't squeal or scowl.

The fairy who sprinkled us was maybe lost
in free thoughts, not long out of fairy school.

What thirsty freedom took over our lips
and how did it offer us the tit to suckle?

When the god trusted me at last to stay
true to his freedom, how did I tip the scale?

In my free nature, half human half creature,
responsibilities turn out to be sexual.

While the god enters the essence of my bones,
I clutch at free meanings wandering round my skull.

Bodies in Mind

He has this body which is mine
and I have another body, his:
one smooth man, one hairy, a chunky
and a scrawny, but with parts that match.
Undressed and ready, they work
on their reciprocal magic, but
I won't embarrass you, friends,
by sharing details in public. How
they suit each other! What each body
has in mind, what each mind needs
from a body, they think and feel.
Bothering each other for fun,
they brazenly examine who is whose,
which you don't ever need to know about.

The Nerves

That pathway of nerves takes me
along my pain and along my pleasure,
from under my depth into my surface,
feathers me up, and screws me back
into myself. I feel through my argument with
the map of my body, find the rumble
under my ears, my tongue licks what's wrong,
my inner stiches pinch. What else can touch me?

And this body is never my own possession, but
it's there when you reach for me and I become
a piece of elastic, a pincushion, a nightingale,
a world of delight awaiting release
when I can say with the nerves:
this is my body, this is my way of using it,
not whole but not empty, though I may feel
empty, though you may feel that I'm whole.

III

Moments

I must lie down where all the ladders start
W. B. YEATS, 'The Circus Animals' Desertion'

Empty Boxes

A seashell has been emptied of its owner, but
a box begins as itself, with a need to enclose.
Was Pandora's box purpose-made, or were
those things shoved into something handy?
The empty box is still somewhere, missing
its ungrateful contents, holding only air.

I have many lovely boxes, too lovely to fill,
like these nifty cigar boxes, some plain wood,
some fancy ones. The man who gave me them
forty years ago, he's been dead for thirty-five:
they screwed his box down tight, afraid
of what they had to put away inside it.

Finding new purposes for boxes takes luck
and judgement, for the size and shape they fit.
Give me shoeboxes and toffee tins, containers
too good to chuck. The shoes and sweets
are elsewhere now, but Pandora's things
will still be jostling us, they mock our boxes.

Effort

Take this prima donna, all strut and froth.
Forget what you can do, it's who you can frighten.

A fair wage for a freak opportunity – afraid
there's nothing left except for the fortunate.

Nature or nurture? Nothing but the fruit.
It can still turn rotten though, for all your effort.

Don't overreach. Take what you can afford
from what gets offered. Why should you go further?

Knowing the cost of it you're shy and furtive,
but unconcern brings off the biggest fraud.

Meet the team. They are unfazed by virtue.
They make us luck. Their ideas keep us fertile.

Monkey has business but thank God it's Friday.
Fuck off and chuck him a nice brass farthing.

Laundry

As I was walking down Higgledy-Piggledy Lane
   I thought I smelt the truth,
that beauty is the answer,
   and the rest is all uncouth.

I opened up my heart to it:
   my heart came back to say,
'Get on and do your laundry,
   this is not a holiday.'

My answer was mechanical
   and gave me little pause:
'I'm in it for the glory
   and the well-deserved applause.

'I want to be the reason
   for the heartbreak of the crowd,
I need to share my beauty.'
   But my heart said, 'Not so loud.

'That isn't any argument
   why anyone should care.
Define the special reason
   why your beauty's even there.'

I blew my nose and cleared my throat
   and made my answer bold:
'I work to make it useless,
   for uselessness is gold.

'You can make it better empty
    than try to make it real;
I like to give the world a thrill
    with what I didn't feel.'

My heart fell silent for a while,
    the weather turned to rain;
I met an ancient washerwoman
    walking up the lane.

She pulled a bottle from her purse
    and took a swig of gin.
'Bugger,' said she, 'My washing's out,
    I'll have to bring it in.'

She brought it in with rainbows
    and my heart leapt up to speak:
'Beauty and truth are what you wear
    because your flesh is weak.

'Your body parts can't get along
    without a helpful soul
to keep them all together
    and to make the substance whole.

'The clinging dirt, and fluids
    that will squirt and seep and smell,
define your truth and beauty
    but you need them clean as well.'

I went into the launderette
   and took off all my clothes.
The washerwoman said to me,
   'You walk around in those?

'I'll wash them for you if you like
   but it will cost you dear,
I'll charge an extra tenner
   for the stink you've brought in here.'

I walked outside quite naked
   and I'm never going back.
I sometimes wear a barrel,
   or a ragged piece of sack,

I shout at you across the street
   as you pass the other side,
'You are your truth, your beauty!
   The answer is inside!'

Royal Worcester

I rattle the crockery a little. Its chime resounds
in time and space and is real. My heart keeps up
the tension to express whatever exists, and look!
Here we are, doing what we do, drinking in
reality out of the special fancy porcelain cups
that are otherwise only left piled up in a sideboard
for the unseen world to keep them, where they're
hard to grasp, missing their actual presence with
the fingers holding the handle, and the lips that sip
on the rim. Life would be a blank without me
to connect thing to thing, and own them as pieces
of myself, as facts. I drink from the very goblet
of the potion that lets me tell you: *Yes, this
is the world we swallow, we take it in, it's ours.*

Bio-Active

Put on your pink rubber gloves and take life
by its molecules – it's a filthy job
and it'll get into you, but that's good!
Dirt is your friend. If you feel lost and lonely
      there's a bacillus for that.

Things grow, they have the fizz and quiver
they need to make themselves what works.
The ginger beer plant wants to know what
you want, its culture is ready and willing
      to sparkle on your tongue.

Everything is alive if you let it live,
it'll make you a moment, a flash of joy,
a deep scoop of the lower depths, a way of making
yourself new every morning, noon and night:
      ask the vinegar mother.

Make me a new person! Make me a loaf,
a posset of coconut milk, a bucket of sauerkraut,
make me understand I'm in thrall,
I belong to existence, I have to make things happen
      because the sourdough says so.

Now Wash Your Hands

I am fidgeting nerve ends, fingertips tapping keyboards,
swiping screens, drumming with nails that secretly grow
from under the skin, that trap grime, that scratch the itch.
I am my touch, and what I touch touches me too.

I am all innocence, unhurt if I'm careful, except that when I
answer what the need is, I'm made dirty. I must save myself
from sin, if sin's what finds me out, when it can make
my righteous soul a viral hive or a bacterial culture.

I am sense in the prints on my pads, in my palm that opens
to close its fist round what it wants – a handrail, a banana,
myself when appropriate: and when I'm satisfied I feel
it's time for me to wipe, clean, wash and refresh who I am.

Moments of Vision

The ultrafuturistic train glides in, and the station
crystallises round it, sparkling marble and sky-blue daylight.

We glide out, the track beneath us imperceptibly smooth;
England is becoming Tuscany by stealth.

The cities opening their windows, the values
evident and shining; we are renewed, resettled.

But it's not all you can do here, gaze at views.
The nightlife! The bars and cafés! Come again at twilight!

The local satisfactions, the nuggets of flavour, pools of joy.
Not for nothing the world's most intelligent toilet.

Knaves are made emperors, the aces are higher
than the angels. Virtue as enticing as adultery.

As you squeeze the toothpaste at bedtime,
you can't fault this day on vision, heart or utility.

Great Moments

A time for banners and processions, shoulders
parading their burdens, a treat for all the children.

Great days in history, beginnings, endings
and decisive moments, the twist, the flip, the jolt.

They haven't emerged for their presentation yet,
I think they must be down there in the shelter.

Red carpets for the great and good. Blue sails
for independent souls, tacking with agility.

White flag for the pure in spirit, somebody
to volunteer for the human shield.

The city hall balcony is still deserted. Caterwauling,
some deranged man who expected socialism.

Frank and to the point, a statement emerges – 'Piss off
with your dirt and fleas, all of you'– from the chairman.

The Swiss consul brushes off his suit and puts it away.
'We shall not be needing formality,' he tells a journalist.

The Runaway Tram
Nikolai Gumilev (1886–1921)

I walked an unfamiliar street
and heard the ravens' sudden scream,
a strumming lute, a thunder peal –
before me loomed a flying tram.

I put my foot upon its platform,
how I did I couldn't say,
and in the air its trails of fire
burned brighter than the light of day.

It rushed like a storm on darkest wings,
lost down a hole in time and sense…
'Stop it, mister tramcar driver,
make this tramcar stop at once!'

Too late. We'd sidled round a wall
and rumbled through a palm-tree grove,
across the Neva, over the Nile,
clattering past the Seine we drove.

And by the window, flashing past,
two penetrating eyes I knew:
that poor old beggar who met his death
down in Beirut a year ago.

Where am I? Troubled and slow, my heart
beats out its answer with a sign:
'Do you see the station where tickets are sold
to travel the Indian Spiritual Line?'

A notice… the bloodstained letters reading
'Greengrocer' – and I can tell
instead of turnips and heads of cabbage,
dead men's heads are what they sell.

In a scarlet shirt, with a face like an udder,
the head-chopper came for me too with his axe
and sliced off my head, which lay with the others
in the slime down here at the bottom of the box.

And yet there's a lane with a picket fence,
a house with three windows, and grass that's grey –
'Stop the tram, mister tramcar driver,
stop this tram at once, I say!'

Máshenka, here you were living and singing,
you wove me a carpet, we plighted our troth,
where are you now, your voice and your figure,
where can you be – have you gone to your death?

How you were sobbing that time in your chamber,
when I in my powder-stiffened coiffure
went to bow down in front of the Empress,
and we would catch sight of each other no more.

I realise now: what freedom we have
comes in from elsewhere on a light breaking through;
people and shadows must wait to go in
at the gates of the interplanetary zoo.

And a breeze springs up, so sweet and familiar,
and flying towards me, from over the bridge,
a rider's hand in a gauntlet of iron
and a couple of hooves that belong to his steed.

Fortress of Orthodox faith, St Isaac's
engraves its profile against the sky.
I'll ask for a service of prayers for Máshenka's
health, and a requiem mass for me.

And still, my heart is mournful for ever,
to breathe is so hard, and it's painful to live...
Máshenka, I would never have thought
it was possible so much to love, and to grieve.

Everything is stony
Vladislav Khodasevich (1886–1939)

Everything is stony. On the stone stairs
night moves along. At gateways and at doors

couples like statues, joined as if they're stuck.
And heavy sighs. Cigars with heavy smoke.

Keys clinked on stone, the bolt clanged in the lock.
You've had to walk the stones till five o'clock.

Wait: piercingly, an ocarina moan
is blown through chinks in lumpy Berlin stone;

behind the houses, ugly morning breaks;
the stepmother of Russian cities wakes.

1923

Better Moments

Alarms and church bells. The old quiet afternoons
long forgotten, the city continues, a flowing solid.

As the earth heaves, the clatter of syllogisms
where it opens up, logic falls and consequences slide.

Farther than ever from hearth and home, planetary craft
explore each other through the observation slits.

The serpent thumbs his nose at the devastated view:
the mountains of the beautiful spite him, turn to salt.

Beyond all this, the musketeers look down at us:
we see them enormous in the sky, three silhouettes.

City in Pieces

How long it takes
        to find pieces of sky,
                pieces of building,
get the edges,
        put them in groups
                in special zones,
make them become
        the cities they are,
                and then eventually
reach somewhere
        you're expected,
                in stories with shapes:
some are vague,
        some are gifted
                with clear limits
making them hard
        but easy cities,
                as life might be
hard to live
        but easy to find.
                You creep around,
look for mountains,
        for magic towers,
                for where to stand.
You've come here
        the strange way,
                finding the edges.
Everything here
        is the case,
                and it creates

poets and painters
                to look at itself.
                        Look up at these
tall steel growths
                out of the land –
                        they are so solid,
sky all around,
                but they have each other.
                        Nothing to fear.
City of cities,
                abode of whoever
                        is blessed with it,
of whoever can
                bless the place,
                        with people inside
who are places too,
                each the end of the
                        end of the earth.
And those who curse it,
                who have lost their
                        taste for the puzzle
or have made it
                a means to their end,
                        make it a place
that has no edges,
                mix up its pieces,
                        throw it up in the air.

In the Dark

I'm still in the dark, but across Europe, dawn
breaks as usual. In a city I visited once, they're
well into breakfast time, and the place around
comes into focus: a significant river,
churches with domes, blocks of flats – blasted,
and daylight is not enough for breakfast.

Morning doesn't always break beyond
the darknesses. One day a dark will cancel
where there were daisies and violets in a field.
What if the cold took over, till everything
turned white, and the eyes couldn't follow
any more where they might have come to.

The dark folds around like a coat. We put it on.
The sea rises millimetres, millimetres,
each crashing wave takes a little more from us
as it falls. Politicians are wasting it all
on their fabric of nothing. The dawn breaks
and the same old hard rain falls all over us.

Ladders and Snakes

I'm superstitious and I'm unbelieving, and
I walk under the ladder – not irrational,
and not unimaginative. Ladders need
to be sound, anchored and used safely.

From square one I've been connected to where
I wander, like all Earth's inhabitants, but
are we attached? Only just, like the handcart
teetering on the slope, ready to roll away.

Monkeys and squirrels in trees play for
all they're worth, hunting and gathering,
can't leave, even in moments of wondering
what can go wrong? Will there be snakes?

The snakes are attached in their way, they need
the friction on bark to give them purchase
so they can climb, though for us they mean
falling, sliding into the hole, the hidden pit.

They can take you down to the blind time
underground, with no progress up the ladders
to the clouds. This life might be freedom, but
where is the life beyond our next move?

IV

Honourable Acts

I had forgiven enough
That had forgiven old age.

W. B. YEATS, 'Quarrel in Old Age'

October Again

Divorce is in the air and nothing looks as wrong
as it ought to. What's new? The neighbours say
there's an owl around in the back gardens, but
I haven't heard it. This year we've been stuck together
too long, but then it's already too many years
we've been stuck together. Trees are shedding,
but only a little, and it's dark earlier now
as October sets in, all as normal. Meanwhile
divorce is occurring, and each of us becomes
more his own self now there's no hard rule against
doing what comes and enjoying it. My other self, my
cousin with the identical name, died a few weeks back
and today I found a photo that I don't remember taking.
I used to joke with him that shaking hands should tilt
the world while we merged into a whole new monster.
My other other self, the one inside me, starts
to do what he wants. Does he care what other people
want him to? Infection in the air, everywhere, that
so far hasn't visited here: neither of us shows
any of the typical symptoms, so we keep on,
stuck being who we are, in each other's way,
and it's October in a different way from the way
it was that stuck us together all those years ago.

Taking Leave

And in the sunset, walking towards the other side
of the neighbourhood, past the avenue of London planes
and under the railway, in this wild glow I can see your glory,
the cherubim and seraphim who guard you, even though
I don't believe they can keep you from harm, your wild scheme
to move beyond the known, at last entered into.
In the sky there's a mess of egg and ketchup, milk and honey.
There's a mention of survival and a hint of loss, of a fact or two
missing. You cried in my arms. Everything is rich
with the unexpected, and worry has left, your grand leap
is beyond fear. It has taken you over the other side
where banks and phone contracts make too much sense.
In the absence of reason, reasons make themselves
like the pointless folding wardrobe you ordered, that
I now get rid of – and I'm bad at getting rid of things.
It's no good expecting your passion channeled into
passages of prose, now there are oracles, volcanoes,
exclamations out of undercurrents of freedom from
everything known. A mind is a capacious suitcase
which can be strapped around, and given to the care
of the baggage handlers. I suppose one day
all thinking will be done like this.

Happy and Fortunate

1. THE BALLET

Out on stage with the scenery and chorus
it's his moment, his life as a dance.

The love interest takes over – her swivelling
en pointe, his perfect leaping bottom. Applause.

This visor is warped, this lance useless,
the innkeeper's mockery – he asked for it.

He has to be rescued, or the story
can't end. It's no way of life, the heroic.

The audience are ready to throw their peanuts.

❧

The box office is closing, no grants from the higher powers,
the stage is unswept and the stagehands go back to their families.

The audience is online only, and the videos are streaming
into the void. How does he get his applause?

Imagination's a balloon, and the helium's escaping.
Nothing can be done. There's only being.

One day the sad man on the stage will have no story left.
We all put on our masks and waltz around the scenery.

2. THE SALLY FORTH

Most happy and fortunate were the days when the bold knight
Don Quixote of La Mancha sallied forth into the world.

Don Quixote, Part I, Chapter 28

Such days of purpose, of great plans and opportunities!
What vision! What passion! What good fortune!

Such is the objective truth pursued by Don Quixote
that every moment will be a triumph of freedom!

Beauty and upright standards are affirmed, his style
makes good the uninhibited effort!

Sancho Panza has his back, despite his own back pain.
He needs to ensure the project will be fruitful.

His schemes will produce something – at least
apples of isolation and plums of forgetfulness.

The reformer of good practice, the maker of decisions
that vindicate, overcome and fortify!

Don't disturb his thinking, he has right and proper
insight into what will take everything further.

He's coming home safely now, held in careful hands
and the work he has done still has scope to be fertile.

Recovery from his expedition may be painful, but
he will continue his mission beyond what life can afford.

This is the story. This is the way of life,
a hope to rescue, and a thorough storming of the fortress.

Horses happen more than
unhappening unicorns.
Does that make
the happening horse matter more?

3. MISTAKES

Don Quixote out in the wild city,
Sancho Panza keeps in touch by email.

If your mistakes are big enough, nobody
has strong enough persuasion, or the right drugs.

Don Quixote in virtual reality,
Sancho Panza in varifocal glasses.

Everything pinging and chiming, the sound
of communication, people existing.

Don Quixote is his own person,
Sancho Panza loses trust in personality.

There's someone in a picture too small
to make out the substance of. Romance occurs.

Don Quixote has plans for his lover,
Sancho Panza weighs the possibilities.

The wanderer at the crossroads needs to think
like the peasant girl at the well, waiting her turn.

Don Quixote in leather jacket and leggings,
Sancho Panza buying shares in corduroy.

There's a swan on the canal, and crows
flit around the cemetery. An owl hoots outside.

Don Quixote with a drone helicopter,
Sancho Panza with a badly drawn bird.

You meet a quantum particle, that tells you:
'It's my own business, get on with your life.'

Don Quixote with a china teaset,
Sancho Panza keeps the keys to the sideboard.

Fields of magnetism, fields of cowpats:
sources of splendour no one understands.

Don Quixote is not afraid of the dark,
Sancho Panza looks for a light bulb.

You've been up late, pacing your insomnia
into the floor, spending your human gift.

Don Quixote makes the party sizzle,
Sancho Panza is too fond of sausages.

The drudge with the jug of milk guides the flow,
but it's the earth that pulls it downwards, to itself.

Don Quixote wants the world to sing,
Sancho Panza hopes it's not too loud.

Do you feel alien? The world upholds you
till you blurt your love for it, and it keeps away.

> *Don Quixote is a free spirit.*
> *Sancho Panza is free too, but heavier.*

You might pick a ticket home safely despite it all,
or they bring you back in handcuffs.

> *Don Quixote makes the news 'And finally',*
> *Sancho Panza puts his phone away.*

4. A Prayer

O commitment! O recovery from disillusion!
What mistakes have I been made to enjoy! Where
is my agency, my persuasion, firm but gentle?

O send me victorious without triumph, set me
in my quiet glory above my self, O bring me
sense without prejudice, a mind free of jaundice.

O soul of a ballerina, of a perfect move across
a notional stage! O gathering of nerve, of power
making steps equivalent to those of a giant!

O so old now! O days of long-wasted moments!
Yet I still require fulfilment when my inner workings
are shot and I won't be able to move my joints!

O for the ancient surprise! O nights of restraint
disregarded, days of crying out loud for God's sake
and the freedom of ungathered chanting!

O days of asparagus and jam! Days of mint tea
and sweetness! Let me deserve my furniture
and aspire to low-dangling chandeliers!

O begin in me! O virtue, I'm making overtures
to you! Perhaps I'm not bound to commit myself
but may I let myself be known by my chintz!

5. Tell Your Story

'Boy, boy,' said Don Quixote in a loud voice, 'tell your
story in a straight line and do not become involved
in curves or transverse lines, for to get a clear idea of
the truth, one must have proofs and more proofs.'
Don Quixote, Part II, Chapter 26

The pudding has to be something he can taste:
it's the reason for eating, or his tongue thinks so.

His cheque book is empty, the millions written out.
Handsome Americans persuade him of his dreams.

A shakeup is needed, a new way to heaven.
In the dark time he can sit still and think.

There's no one way to tell him, and in fact
there may be no way at all, now he's enchanted.

Making a hash of his life has left the story hanging.
The proof of your sanity is in telling it straight.

6. Up and Down

'The tambourine's in just the right hands,' responded Sancho Panza.

Don Quixote Part II, Chapter 22

Up is yes, and the answer to a good many questions.
Everybody knows it, it goes with please and thankyou.

Raise up your tambourine as you bash it,
shout to disturb their first class dining-car.

Bottled energy is your up, bottled sleep is your down:
it's good to know you can rely on a gin and tonic.

The Don and Sancho leave the room to the enchanters,
three of them: next they will work on the donkey.

The chief enchanter lowers his eyes and sighs deeply:
the charm is wrong, nothing but glamour and twinkle.

Sancho Panza has rotundity to keep him together,
Don Quixote's armour rattles round his tunic.

Descend to the bottom for a transformational dream.
Forget your way back, there's more of the maze than you think.

Don Quixote is down inspecting the drains,
Sancho Panza up in the loft, looking for holes in the tank.

7. ALPHABET

Don Quixote jumps over the quick brown fox,
Sancho Panza is lying doggo.

Don Quixote jovially wakes his buff groom Sancho Panza.
Sancho Panza vows jokily to forget Don Quixote, the bum.

Don Quixote may live his job,
Sancho Panza works in fog.

Don Quixote kicks a high jive in a lumpy borrowed fez,
Sancho Panza's wedged trilby fixes unique joky moves.

Don Quixote believes in magic,
Sancho Panza in works of joy.

Don Quixote's borrowed fez is caught up in killjoy moths,
Sancho Panza's rhythms quiver and flex, wake the jaded bugs.

Don Quixote loves jiffy bags.
Sancho Panza worms okay.

Don Quixote bravely fakes a slow champagne jizz,
Sancho Panza just videos my Queer as Folk wig box.

Don Quixote fucks your mum,
Sancho Panza gives blowjobs.

Don Quixote's humble joke: crazy vape goes woof.
Sancho Panza's quiet brag: woke move fixed jelly.

Don Quixote moves to Fiji.
Sancho Panza: Walk or buggy?

The horses are
each other's whisperer:
their fear is acknowledged but
it keeps down in a corner of the field
by itself.

8. THE STRUGGLE

Don Quixote is opening a new front in the struggle,
facing new ways to experience depression and stress.

Sancho Panza has made a vow, solemn and simple,
to feed his hunger and slake his terrible thirst.

It's now Thursday. Time to wash the dishes
and sacrifice a duck to the gods of drizzle.

'Is your journey really necessary?' people ask.
Don Quixote and Sancho Panza wait on the terrace.

Everything has become new and fresh since the Duchess
made her entrance in a diamanté dress.

Dinner is coming soon. There will be wine
and we must observe the smiles of the waitress.

After dinner, the speeches. But there's no blame
if everyone starts feeling a little drowsy.

Once the music stops and the guests are departing,
Don Quixote will stand up and declare a truce.

9. HONOURABLE ACTS

'Now I believe,' said Don Quixote at this point, 'what I have
believed on many other occasions: the enchanters who pursue
me simply place figures as they really are before my eyes, and
then change and alter them into whatever they wish.'

Don Quixote, Part II, Chapter 28

This is a humorous tale of false consciousness,
the loss of faculties, and inhibition thrown to the winds.

Don Quixote has paid his way in honourable acts
and now he has left the enchanted castle keep.

Everything about money is left to the others
who will know how to satisfy the innkeepers.

A cup of fennel tea for Sancho Panza, he needs
to recover some dignity after such wandering.

Sweep out the fluff, the gullibility, disenchant
the deluded, stop them being ridiculous!

But ridiculousness is necessary. They may fail
to survive outside this empty box of tricks.

Often I muse on Don Quixote and his hope, his faith,
his charity. I no longer laugh at Sancho Panza.

Forget the Rest

        We made our peace, or did we?
Not that I feel we did. So what do I
do now? If we
        were ever going to make a new
list of what we needed, how would we
even agree
        together any bit of it? There's
more of this. There's too much time
to waste on what
        I never felt was mine, but we
have separate lives. And here I sit
waiting for something – I
        forget what. Two of us
making little progress, if there's ever
progress in
        the afterlife of what's been
done. I couldn't have guessed the end,
but there's no end, the
        rest is jabbering on
until there'll be no more, but
we were together. I forget the rest.

Across a Field

Sometimes it's the field across which life is not a walk.
Sometimes it's the way home but not yet.
Picking blackberries as you go needs you to bring
a plastic bag or a bucket to collect them in.

Not that I mean to go on for ever like this,
but places are destinations only when you stop.
Home is a point of departure, too. Nowhere is
anywhere, and somewhere is where you are now.

Dormouse Summer

When one subtracts from life infancy (which is vegetation), sleep,
eating and swilling, buttoning and unbuttoning – how much
remains of downright existence? The summer of a dormouse.

Byron, Journal 7 December 1813

Missing the small moment of warmth
and possibility: is it the greatest fault?

What I do to maintain myself: a few
habits of solitude and unbundled filth.

Buttoning and unbuttoning, the clothes
make their own time, expandable and fluid.

What is history but a straw in the wind,
a bird making a nest, a toot on a flute.

Existing for its own sake: how many moments
make up this tiny summer as it folds?

I can eat my own weight over again,
I can become a giant in my own field.

Sleep has a call on life: is it the genuine
purpose, to build a darkness where we float?

'That's the secret,' says the dormouse,
'Falling into the void is the start of flight.'

Sawdust

Once I thought I saw my own transparent
self, but where has it gone? Now it's all
darkness and untoward imaginings of
what I didn't do. I remember nothing
        but sawdust and straw.

If you've gone with the spoons, mind of mine,
wait for me over where the world reveals
what's underneath. If it's not there after all,
you can ignore me, abandon me, and down
        into the teapot I go.

I'd like there to be a souvenir of what was
all so straightforward, some last element
of fact. Leave a little shit behind in the bowl,
put your gum on the banister, a footprint
        on the priceless carpet.

Braggart of no achievement, dandy prancing
along the pier over the edge, get lost and then
I won't mind because you know anything goes
when you've gone. For all that, I'll regret
        our passing, you and me.

Waiting In It

Waiting in it: this is not a room with a view, nor
a room of one's own, nor a philosopher's boudoir.

After the discoveries of where: the what to be,
the how, the who, the when. The clay for the potter.

I find my strength in a pure flow towards the light
making me able to shine a little better.

A few imperfect gestures, a garden to sit in:
a feather and a leaf as an example, a pattern.

I wait here, listening, a hollow vessel, yet
I enjoy an identity. I am a being. I am Peter.

Acknowledgements and Notes

Many thanks to members of workshops – the Torriano group, and groups led by Katy Evans-Bush and Kate Bingham – for thorough examination of poems at early stages; and further to Katy Evans-Bush for thoughts on how the collection would fit together, and to Gregory Woods and Jacqueline Saphra for reading it.

Thanks to editors of magazines who have taken my poems from their unmanageable slush piles. Poems here have been published in *Butcher's Dog, High Window, Impossible Archetype, Ink Sweat & Tears, London Grip, Long Poem Magazine, New Walk, Perverse, Prole, Snowflake.*

Some poems go back a while: an early version of 'Pastoral Interlude' appeared in *Peacock Luggage* (1992), and 'Prodigal Son' was in *Through the Bushes* (2000), both Smith/Doorstop.

Thank you W. B. Yeats for lending me the key to the book.

Don Quixote quotes are from Edith Grossman's translation.

Old joke: 'My mother made me a homosexual.' 'If I gave her the wool, would she make me one?'

'We were together, I forget the rest' is a popular meme derived from Walt Whitman's 'Once I Pass'd Through a Populous City', 'Day by day and night by night we were together – all else has long been forgotten by me', somehow crossed with Robert Browning's 'Memorabilia':

> For there I picked up on the heather
> And there I put inside my breast
> A moulted feather, an eagle-feather –
> Well, I forget the rest.

The Russian proverb 'Life is not a walk across a field' is the last line of Boris Pasternak's poem 'Hamlet'.

This book has been typeset by
SALT PUBLISHING LIMITED
using Sabon, a font designed by Jan Tschichold
for the D. Stempel AG, Linotype and Monotype Foundries.
It is manufactured using Holmen Book Cream 70gsm,
a Forest Stewardship Council™ certified paper from the
Hallsta Paper Mill in Sweden. It was printed and bound
by Clays Limited in Bungay, Suffolk, Great Britain.

SHEFFIELD
GREAT BRITAIN
MMXXIV